Managing Your Mind While Saving Others:

A First Responder's Guide to Vicarious Trauma

LaLisa Morgan, LCSW

This book demonstrates an impressive personal improvement tool. It is not a substitute for working with qualified licensed clinical staff in psychotherapy. Nothing contained herein is meant to replace qualified legal, medical, or mental health advice. The author urges the reader to use these techniques under the supervision of a qualified therapist or physician. The author and publisher do not assume responsibility for how the reader chooses to apply the techniques herein. Readers are advised to consult with their physician, attorney, or other licensed professional practitioner before implementing any suggestions that follow. This book is not intended to take the place of sound professional advice, legal, medical, mental, or otherwise. Neither the author nor the publisher assumes any liability for possible adverse consequences because of the information constrained within.

www.kingdomjourney4life.com
www.kingdomjourney2healing.com

Book Overview: **Managing Your Mind While Saving Others: A First Responder's Guide to Vicarious Trauma** was written for First Responders to gain approaches to maximize success while managing real life with sound mental health practices. First Responders, such as Law Enforcement, Child Welfare Social Workers, Ambulance Staff, Emergency Room Nurses and Doctors, Licensed Therapists, Security Professionals, and other professionals are often the people who assist people in a crisis. These individuals are the "helpers" of society to stabilize the community and keep the community safe. Trauma is a costly, public health issue. By addressing your own healing, you can greatly impact healing in your family and the community as a first responder. By reading this book, the reader will:

- Define mental health being a First Responder impacts both your professional and personal relationships are affecting your mental health.
- Learn about chronic stress, burnout, and vicarious trauma and how it impacts your quality of life.
- Align your core values with your self-care plan.
- Set boundaries with family, friends, and emergency response partners to build a healthy professional practice.
- Create your wellness strategies and maximize your mental wellness as you create the life-work balance.

First published March 2024
Hardcover
ISBN: 9798321068403
Imprint: Independently published

Dedication:

**This book and the principles I learned are dedicated to the Los Angeles County Department of Children and Family Services, Emergency Response Command Post Team--Social Workers and Supervisors in Los Angeles County.
You are the gatekeepers of child safety. Unsung First Responders of our community. Take care of yourself.**

Table of Contents

Managing Your Mind While Saving Others:

First Responder's Guide to Vicarious

There are more than <u>160 million</u> people who are a part of the U.S. workforce today.

U.S. Bureau of Labor Statistics. (2022). Table A-1: Employment Status of civilian population by sex and age. Retrieved from: https://www.bls.gov/news.release/empsit.t01.htm

Mental Health Statistics by Gender

- More than one in five women in the U.S. experienced a mental health condition in the last year. Certain mental health conditions, like depression and bipolar disorder, affect more women than men.
- In fact, the prevalence of any mental illness was higher among women (27.2%) than men (18.1%) in 2021.
- Over 6 million men in the U.S. experience depression each year. Men are more likely to report symptoms such as fatigue, irritability, and loss of interest in work or hobbies rather than feelings of sadness or worthlessness.
- 19.1 million adults in the U.S. ages 19 to 54 experience an anxiety disorder, and more than 3 million men experience panic disorder, agoraphobia, or other phobias.
- 90% of individuals diagnosed with schizophrenia by age 30 are men.
- Men account for approximately 10% of patients who experience anorexia or bulimia and 35% of those who experience a binge eating disorder. Men are less likely to seek professional help for an eating disorder than women.

https://www.forbes.com/health/mind/mental-health-statistics/#:~:text=How%20Many%20People%20Experience%20Mental%20Health%20Issues%3F%201,to%20246%20million%2C%20which%20is%20about%2028%25.%20; Accessed 3/19/2024.

"Mental health in the workplace: It's not a nice-to-have, it's a must-have."

Human Resources Leader and Business Consultant

National Alliance on Mental Health reports that
"1 in 5 US Adults Experience Mental Illness"

"Mental Health By The Numbers"

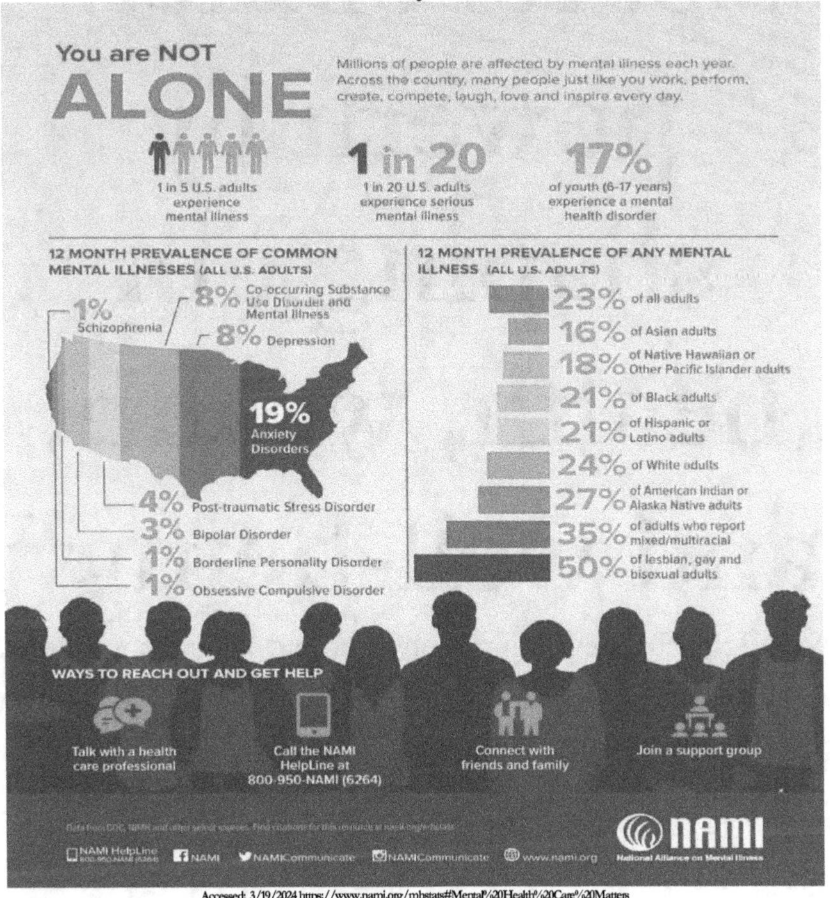

Accessed: 3/19/2024 https://www.nami.org/mhstats#Mental%20Health%20Care%20Matters

"<u>Work </u>is one of the most vital parts of life, powerfully shaping our health, wealth, and well-being"

Well Being In the Nation Network. (n.d.). Vital conditions.
Retrieved from https:// winnetwork.org/vital-conditions

The mental health at work study revealed that <u>76%</u> of respondents reported

at <u>least one symptom of a mental health condition,</u> an increase of 17 percentage points in just two years

Mind Share Partners. (2021).
2021 Mental health at work report—the stakes have
been raised.

https://www.mindsharepartners.org/mentalhealthatworkreport-2021

First Responders carry the weight of our tragedies and transform it into hope.

Author Unknown

PREFACE: WHO IS A FIRST RESPONDER?

The Homeland Security Act of 2002 defines First Responders as individuals who protect life, evidence, property or the environment during the early stages of an emergency (www.dhs.gov). The term "first responder" includes a firefighter, law enforcement officer, paramedic, emergency medical technician, child abuse investigators, or other individuals, government or community based, and sometimes volunteer, who, in the course of his or her professional duties, responds to fire, medical, hazardous material, or other similar emergencies. As First Responders, we are often the first in and last to leave an emergency. The "situation" can be intense, stressful, and full of many activities, and it often occurs because of violence, abuse, neglect, loss, disaster, war, and other emotionally harmful experiences. First Responders are often passionate about the work you do. However, this type of role can take a toll on you over time. You are human after all.

You lead by example. You try to live your life in a way that reflects the values that you hold dear. Whether it's by volunteering in your community, being kind to strangers, or standing up for what you believe in, you hope that your actions can serve as a positive example for others. You listen to others. Sometimes, all someone needs are a listening ear. You try to be present and attentive when someone is sharing their struggles with you and offer support and encouragement when you can.

I wrote this book initially as a reminder to myself. I have been a First Responder for over seventeen years now. There was a time I forgot to love and take care of me. I graciously learned to forgive myself and love me again. I learned to set health boundaries as I embraced who I was as a human being first.

I have worked with law enforcement, fire fighters, ambulance responders, nurses, doctors, and security personnel all responsible for being the first to maintain order and bring stabilization and safety to a situation. I have also watched these same individuals live a life whereas they suffer silently. The families fall apart. They quietly fall deeper into depression.

I have watched professionals treat each other with disrespect or they are just plain mean. I have had discussions with people who don't pay attention to their financial means and don't have enough money to retire working past retirement age. Or they work because they have failed to keep healthy attachments with their kids or other family members. First Responders deserve a quality life. Many First Responders deny their own mental health needs. At one time, I denied my own. I am approaching my half century birthday when this book is published. I have been reflecting on what I have missed out on by not taking care of myself. This book reflects the past two years of study on what it means to take care of me! I share this journey with you so that your next years on this earth are prosperous, joyful and full of the boundaries you need to set for your own journey. May this book start the path for you healing.

LaLisa Morgan, LCSW
Author, Therapist, & Speaker

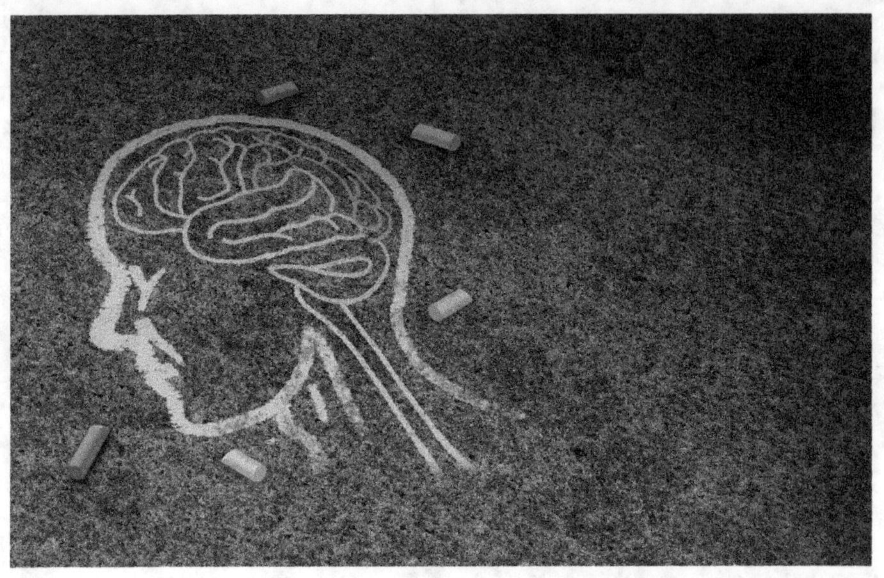

It is important to prioritize your mental health.

FIRST RESPONDERS ARE PULLED IN TOO MANY DIRECTIONS

First Responders are pulled in so many directions and into everyone's business. You have multiple roles: husband, father, wife, mother, grandmother/grandfather, church member, community activist, aunt, and many others. Surviving the chaos of life through our roles and responsibilities can seem like an uphill battle. We desire to help others. We desire peace in our communities. The problem is how can we achieve the best version of ourselves and... manage everyone else's stuff... especially the work-related stress... workplace politics... and whatever else life throws at us?

The Homeland Security Act of 2002 defines First Responders as individuals who protect life, evidence, property, or the environment during the early stages of an emergency (www.dhs.gov). The term "first responder" includes a firefighter, law enforcement officer, paramedic, emergency medical technician, child abuse investigators, or other individuals, government or community based, and sometimes volunteer, who, during his or her professional duties, responds to fire, medical, hazardous material, or other similar emergencies. As First Responders, we are often the first in and last to leave an emergency. The "situation" can be intense, stressful, and full of many activities, and it often occurs because of violence, abuse, neglect, loss, disaster, war, and other emotionally harmful experiences. First Responders are often passionate about the work you do. However, this type of role can take a toll on you over time. You are human after all. Minding your mental health and being aware of vicarious trauma will help you be a better human being to yourself, your family, and the community you love. Ideally, your work as a First Responder should align with your core values and beliefs as well as help you maintain better health and better professional relationships. It is important to prioritize your mental well-being.

First Responders, such as Law Enforcement, Child Welfare Social Workers, Ambulance Staff, Emergency Room Nurses and Doctors, Licensed Therapists, and other professionals are often the people who assist people in a crisis. These individuals are the "helpers" of society to stabilize the community and keep the community safe. Trauma is a costly, public health issue. It occurs because of violence, abuse, neglect, loss, disaster, war, and other emotionally harmful experiences. Trauma does cross all boundaries and reaches everyone without regard to race, age, gender, socioeconomic status, ethnicity, geography, or sexual orientation. ***Trauma is a behavioral health problem, and the solution is mental wellness and helping people find their "why" and "balance in living life.***

The term vicarious trauma sometimes also called compassion fatigue or secondary trauma, is the latest term that describes the phenomenon generally associated with the "cost of caring" for others. That is why First Responders are often the people who suffer in silence, and this impacts not only the individual, however, as an issue of public regard, their families, and children too. First Responders may have also experienced in their personal lives through ongoing relationship issues, including a history of generational trauma. Many First Responders go through the trauma and drama of life and never truly healed. First Responders need to care for themselves better to strengthen families, build the community, and ensure the public safety.

Mental health can best be described by your relationship with yourself, the people you love, and the people in the community—**RELATIONSHIPS**. Relationship is how all human beings react to the world around the individual. Relationships validate our humanity and as a result, are a part of your mental health. The evidence of good mental health is mastering your emotions. Bad mental health is displayed through poor relationships with yourself (examples include suicidal thoughts, depression, and anxiety), poor communication with coworkers and managers, broken communication with family and friends, and significant mental health decline. A great solution to managing poor mental health can be discovered in the process of ***Mental Health Therapy.*** Mental health therapy is a form of treatment used to help people manage and cope with mental health issues and social and relationship problems. It typically involves talking to a therapist about your experiences, thoughts, and feelings, to gain insight and learn positive coping strategies. It is paid for on a cash basis or by medical insurance. Private Pay therapy protects your privacy the best. ***Using medical insurance, your life insurance policy will verify with***

your health insurance records. Do not be discouraged from getting the help you need. This is information for you to maximize your life insurance by paying privately to ensure the funding you want on your policy.

Despite how you pay for therapy, mental health therapy, you can gain the skills and confidence to better understand and manage the challenges that arise in life, especially, workplace trauma (vicarious trauma or compassion fatigue). By managing your emotions, you make sound decisions as a healthy human being. Mental health therapy can be extremely helpful in helping people to better manage their mental health. It can provide a safe and supportive environment where people can discuss their feelings and experiences and learn to identify and regulate their emotions. It can also provide tools and strategies to help people cope with difficult situations, better manage stress, and build resilience. Ultimately, mental health therapy can help people to feel more in control of their overall health and well-being and lead a more fulfilling and meaningful life as a First Responder.

Achieving emotional mastery or mastering your emotions is an important part of being a First Responder.

Mastering your emotions is a crucial aspect of self-improvement and personal growth. Emotions can often be overwhelming and can cause us to react impulsively, which can lead to negative consequences. One such negative consequence has been workplace violence.

Workplace violence is the act or threat of violence, ranging from verbal abuse to physical assaults directed toward persons at work or on duty. The impact of workplace violence can range from psychological issues to physical injury, or even death. Violence can occur in any workplace and among any type of worker, but the risk for fatal violence is greater for workers in sales, protective services, and transportation, while the risk for nonfatal violence resulting in days away from work is greatest for healthcare and social assistance workers.

Workplace violence encompasses a range of behavior, from verbal abuse to physical attacks, directed at individuals while at work or on duty. The ramifications of workplace violence can vary from psychological trauma to physical harm, and even death. While violence can occur in any workplace and among any worker, some are more vulnerable than others. For instance, those in sales, protective services, and transportation face a higher risk of fatal violence, while healthcare and social assistance workers are more likely to experience nonfatal violence leading to time away from work. The Center for Disease Control indicates that workplace violence is a serious issue that affects millions of workers worldwide. It not only poses a significant threat to the personal safety of employees but also has a negative impact on the overall productivity and morale of the workplace.

First Responders and their employers have a legal and ethical responsibility to provide a safe and secure work environment for themselves and the people who work for the company. This includes taking proactive steps to prevent workplace violence and providing support to those who have been affected by it. The risk of workplace violence can be higher in certain industries and job roles. For example, workers in healthcare, social assistance, and customer service are often at a higher risk of facing violent situations due to the nature of their work.

It is important for First Responders to take their safety seriously. Additionally, Employers have a duty to train their employees on how to recognize and respond to potential violent situations. This can include de-escalation techniques, conflict resolution strategies, and emergency response protocols. Employers can also take physical security measures to prevent workplace violence, such as installing security cameras, limiting access to certain areas, and providing consistent security personnel.

In the event of a violent incident, it is crucial for First Responders, employers, managers, and staff to have a clear and effective crisis response plan in place. This includes notifying law enforcement, providing medical attention to those who are injured, and offering support to affected employees. Most importantly, First Responders and their Employers have a **DUTY** to protect healthy mental health practices in both a personal and professional manner. Employers especially should also prioritize access to Employee Related Mental Health Support. This impacts the well-being of First Responders and other employees who have been affected by workplace violence. This can include providing access to counseling services and creating a supportive work environment. By taking proactive steps to prevent and respond to workplace violence, First Responders can create a safer and more secure work environment for their co-workers. First Responders will need to master your emotions to ensure workplace safety. On your journey towards emotional mastery, you may want to reflect on the following:

- Identify your emotions: Before you can master your emotions, you need to be able to identify them. Take the time to reflect on how you are feeling and try to pinpoint the underlying emotions behind your reactions.

- Practice self-awareness: Self-awareness is key to emotional mastery. Take the time to notice how your emotions are affecting your thoughts, behavior, and physical sensations.

- Use mindfulness techniques: Mindfulness techniques can help you stay present and aware of your emotions in the moment. Techniques such as deep breathing, meditation, and yoga can be effective in helping you manage your emotions.

- Practice empathy: Empathy is the ability to understand and share the feelings of others. By practicing empathy, you can better understand the emotions of those around you, which can help you regulate your own emotions.

- Develop healthy coping mechanisms: Everyone experiences negative emotions from time to time. It is important to develop healthy coping mechanisms that can help you manage these emotions in a positive way. This could include things like exercise, talking to a friend, or engaging in a creative activity.

If you are struggling to master your emotions on your own, don't hesitate to seek professional help. You can contact a community mental health provider in your local area or by going to www.kingdomjourney4life.com. A therapist or counselor can provide you with the tools and support you need to manage your emotions effectively.

First Responders, including social workers and licensed therapists, working with trauma survivors can also experience vicarious trauma because of the work they do. Vicarious trauma is the emotional residue of exposure that counselors have from working with people as they are hearing their trauma stories and become witnesses to the pain, fear, and terror that trauma survivors have endured.

BE THE CHANGE YOU WANT TO SEE IN THE WORLD!!

AUTHOR UNKNOWN

BURNOUT VERSUS VICARIOUS TRAUMA

It is important not to confuse vicarious trauma with "burnout". Vicarious trauma, also known as compassion fatigue or secondary traumatic stress, is a common condition that develops when people who are continuously exposed to others' traumatic experiences exhibit symptoms related to trauma. Professions such as law enforcement, social work, healthcare, and counseling are particularly vulnerable to vicarious trauma as they interact with trauma-affected individuals regularly. Symptoms of vicarious trauma include anxiety, depression, a feeling of helplessness, and a reduced ability to empathize with others. First Responders must be aware of the signs of vicarious trauma in themselves and members of their team and provide the necessary support and resources to prevent its negative effects on mental health and job performance.

Burnout in the workplace is a state of physical, emotional, and mental exhaustion caused by prolonged and excessive stress. It is a condition that affects people across all industries and can have a significant impact on their overall well-being. Burnout can be caused by a variety of factors, including work-related stressors, such as long hours, high workloads, and a lack of support or resources.

Chronic stress in the workplace is a type of ongoing stress that arises from various factors such as high workload, long working hours, conflicts with colleagues or superiors, lack of support, and job insecurity. Unlike acute stress, which is a normal response to a challenging situation, chronic stress is persistent and can lead to physical, mental, and emotional exhaustion over time. It can also affect job performance, relationships with colleagues, and overall quality of life. The effects of chronic stress in the workplace can be detrimental to both the individual and the organization, and it is essential to identify and manage it effectively to prevent burnout and promote well-being.

Burnout is generally something that happens over time, usually chronic stress, and as it builds up a change, such as time off or a new and sometimes different job, can take care of burnout or improve it. Vicarious trauma, however, is a state of tension and preoccupation of the stories/trauma experiences described by clients.

It is common to hear people talk about feeling "stressed," "burned out" or experiencing "trauma." While these terms may seem similar, they refer to two distinct phenomena. Burnout is a state of emotional, physical, and mental exhaustion caused by excessive and prolonged stress, often related to work. Vicarious trauma, on the other hand, is a form of indirect trauma that occurs when an individual is exposed to the traumatic experiences of others, such as clients, patients, or loved ones. Here are some key differences between chronic stress, burnout, and vicarious trauma:

Chronic Stress:

- Overwhelming workloads
- Long hours
- Lack of support or resources
- High levels of pressure and responsibility

- The symptoms of burnout can manifest in various ways, including decreased productivity, increased negativity, physical symptoms, and social withdrawal.

Burnout:

- Difficulty concentrating and making decisions
- Exhaustion and a lack of energy
- Cynicism and negativity towards work
- Physical symptoms such as headaches and stomachaches
- Increased use of alcohol or drugs as a coping mechanism
- Withdrawal from social interactions
- Often occurs because of work-related stress
- Can affect anyone in any profession or industry
- Is characterized by emotional exhaustion, cynicism, and a reduced sense of personal accomplishment
- Can lead to physical symptoms such as headaches, insomnia, and chronic fatigue
- May be prevented or mitigated by self-care practices such as exercise, mindfulness, and regular breaks

Vicarious trauma:

- Occurs because of exposure to traumatic events experienced by others
- Is common among helping professionals such as therapists, social workers, and First Responders

- Is characterized by intrusive thoughts, emotional numbing, and a sense of helplessness or despair
- Can lead to physical symptoms such as sleep disturbances and gastrointestinal issues
- May be prevented or mitigated by self-awareness, supervision, and therapy

It's important to recognize the differences between chronic stress, burnout, and vicarious trauma, as they require different approaches to prevention and treatment. While burnout may be alleviated by taking a break or engaging in self-care activities, vicarious trauma often requires more specialized support and intervention. By understanding these distinctions, we can better support ourselves and those around us who may be experiencing these challenges. This tension and preoccupation might be experienced by First Responders in several ways. As a First Responder, you may experience the following:

- Avoid talking or thinking about what the trauma effected client(s) have been talking about, almost being numb to it
- Be in a persistent arousal state
- Having difficulty talking about their feelings
- Free floating anger and/or irritation
- Startle effect/being jumpy

- Over-eating or under-eating
- Difficulty falling asleep and/or staying asleep
- Losing sleep over patients
- Worried that they are not doing enough for their clients
- Dreaming about their clients/their clients' trauma experiences
- Diminished joy toward things they once enjoyed
- Feeling trapped by their work as a counselor (crisis counselor)
- Diminished feelings of satisfaction and personal accomplishment
- Dealing with intrusive thoughts of clients with especially severe trauma histories
- Feelings of hopelessness associated with their work/clients
- Blaming others

Vicarious trauma can impact a First Responders' professional performance and function, as well as result in errors in judgment and mistakes. Vicarious trauma, also known as secondary trauma, is a type of trauma experienced by individuals who are exposed to the traumatic experiences of others. In the case of First Responders, they are often exposed to traumatic events on a regular basis, which can take a toll on their mental health and well-being. Some of the ways vicarious trauma can impact a First Responder's professional performance and function include:

- **Impaired decision-making:** First Responders who are experiencing vicarious trauma may struggle to make sound decisions in high-pressure situations. They may second-guess themselves or hesitate, which can result in mistakes or delays that could have serious consequences.

- **Emotional exhaustion**: Constant exposure to traumatic events can lead to emotional exhaustion, leaving First Responders feeling drained and unable to cope with the demands of their job. This can lead to burnout, which can be difficult to recover from.

- **Difficulty with relationships:** First Responders who are experiencing vicarious trauma may struggle with maintaining healthy relationships with their colleagues, friends, and family members. They may become withdrawn or irritable, which can strain their relationships and make it difficult to receive the support they need.

- **Physical symptoms:** Vicarious trauma can also manifest in physical symptoms such as headaches, insomnia, and digestive issues. These physical symptoms can further exacerbate the emotional and mental toll of vicarious trauma.

It's important for First Responders to recognize the signs of vicarious trauma and seek support when needed. This may include talking to a therapist, participating in peer support groups, or taking time off work to prioritize self-care. By prioritizing their mental health, First Responders can better serve their communities and fulfill their professional duties. Here are some self-evaluation behaviors that you may want to reflect on your life experiences:

Behavior Observations:
- Frequent job changes
- Tardiness
- Free floating anger/irritability
- Absenteeism
- Irresponsibility
- Overwork
- Irritability
- Exhaustion
- Talking to oneself (a critical symptom)
- Increased Isolation from family or friends
- Going out to avoid being alone
- Dropping out of community affairs
- Rejecting physical and emotional closeness

Interpersonal Observations:

- Staff conflict
- Blaming others
- Conflictual engagement
- Poor relationships
- Poor communication
- Impatience
- Avoidance of working with clients with trauma histories
- Lack of collaboration
- Withdrawal and isolation from colleagues
- Change in relationship with colleagues
- Difficulty having rewarding relationships

Personal values/beliefs changes:

- Dissatisfaction
- Negative perception
- Loss of interest
- Apathy
- Blaming others
- Lack of appreciation
- Lack of interest and caring
- Detachment
- Hopelessness
- Low self-image
- Worried about not doing enough
- questioning their frame of reference – identity, world view, and/or spirituality
- Disruption in self-capacity (ability to maintain positive sense of self, ability to modulate strong affect, and/or ability to maintain an inner sense of connection)
- Disruption in needs, beliefs, and relationships (safety, trust, esteem, control, and intimacy)

Job Performance:

- Low motivation
- Increased errors
- Decreased quality
- Avoidance of job responsibilities
- Over-involved in details/perfectionism
- Defensiveness
- Lack of flexibility

The goal of knowing these symptoms is to get help. Vicarious trauma can also impact a First Responders' personal life, such as relationships with family and friends, as well as the first responder's overall health and well-being, which includes both emotional health and physical health. If you are struggling with connections with other people, have complicated work drama, or difficulty with mastering your emotions on your own, don't hesitate to seek professional help. Life coaches, although helpful, are not qualified therapist. A therapist or counselor can provide you with the tools and support you need to manage your emotions effectively. Submit an inquiry for a free 15-minute consultation with LCSW LaLisa Morgan at info@kingdomjourney4life.com or someone licensed as a therapist in your area (www.psychologytoday.com). If you have experienced any of these traumatic events, please consider a conversation with a licensed therapist. ***Licensed therapists include:***

- Licensed Clinical Social Worker (LCSW)
- Licensed Professional Counselor (LPC)
- Marriage and Family Therapist (MFT)
- Associate Clinical Social Worker (ACSW)
- Marriage and Family Therapist Intern (MFTI)
- Psychologist

Other Professionals you may find are:

- Psychiatrists
- Pastoral Counselors
- Certified Peer Specialist
- Alcohol & Drug Abuse Counselor
- Domestic Violence Counselors

You are never alone as you deal with life issues. You should not expect yourself to be perfect. We all make mistakes, and we all experience some level of sadness. Talk Therapy is a tool that can be used to figure out things and help us see when we are stuck in defense mechanisms that are trying to keep ourselves safe. Take care of yourself and access the right person. The goal is find balance in everything we do.

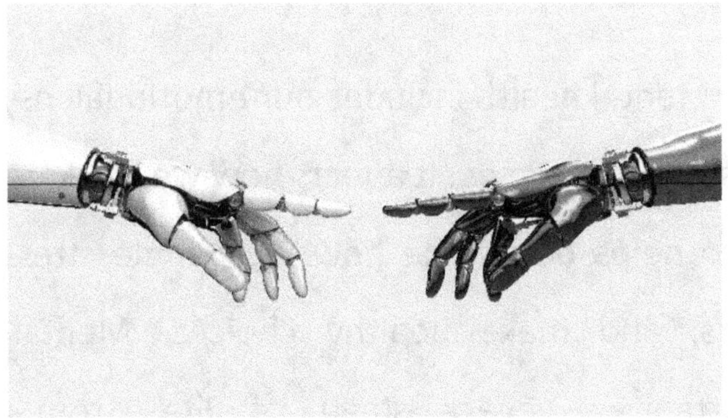

It's okay to

ask for help.

TRAUMA INFORMED FIRST RESPONDER

Mental health includes our emotional, psychological, and social well-being. It affects how we think, feel, and act. It also helps determine how we handle stress, relate to others, and make healthy choices. Mental health is important at every stage of life, from childhood, adolescence, adulthood, and all the way to the end stages of life. Although the terms are often used interchangeably, poor mental health and mental illness are not the same. A person can experience poor mental health and not be diagnosed with a mental illness. Likewise, a person diagnosed with a mental illness can experience periods of physical, mental, and social well-being.

Mental illnesses are among the most common health conditions in the United States. More than 50% will be diagnosed with a mental illness or disorder at some point in their lifetime. One in five Americans will experience a mental illness each year. One in five children, either currently or at some point during their life, have had a seriously debilitating mental illness. One in 25 Americans lives with a serious mental illness, such as schizophrenia, bipolar disorder, or major depression. First Responders can and will develop significant mental health conditions that impact your relationship with yourself, your family, and your environment.

The COVID-19 pandemic had a major effect on our lives. Many of us are facing challenges that can be stressful and overwhelming in our business and in our family life. Learning to cope with stress in a healthy way will help you, the people you care about, and those around you become more resilient. Stress is a physical and emotional reaction that people experience as they encounter challenges in life. When you're under stress, your body reacts by releasing hormones that produce the "fight-or-flight" response.

Job stress can be defined as the harmful physical and emotional responses that occur when the requirements of the job do not match the capabilities, resources, or needs of the worker. Job stress can lead to poor health and even injury. Stress can cause the following:

- Feelings of fear, anger, sadness, worry, numbness, or frustration

- Changes in appetite, energy, desires, and interests

- Difficulty concentrating and making decisions

- Nightmares or problems sleeping

- Physical reactions, such as headaches, body pains, stomach problems, or skin rashes

- Worsening of chronic health problems and mental health conditions

- Increased use of alcohol, illegal drugs (like heroin, cocaine, methamphetamine), and misuse of prescription drugs (like opioids)

It is your business as a First Responder to take care of yourself. You can't give from an empty cup. First Responders need to be aware of how to support your colleagues and mostly yourself, to ensure that receive the right assistance and care. Many of the families we serve have had chronic exposure to trauma or traumatic experiences.

What is a Vicarious Trauma Informed First Responder?

A Vicarious Trauma-Informed First Responder recognizes the challenges of exposure to the trauma experiences of others as an occupational challenge in the field of victim services (such as Law Enforcement, Medical and Child Welfare personnel) and proactively addresses the impact of vicarious trauma through policies, procedures, practices, and programs. You are a First Responder who makes it a priority to take care of yourself and others by making sure policies protect the workers. First Responders with Trauma as described in this book often have complex trauma. First Responders have the needs for their own families and trauma history can impact Staff Turnover in First Responder roles. The truth is, both the agency and the First Responders need to take mental health seriously. The agency can have worries about vicarious trauma and its workforce. This can include:

- Organizational Health-Vicarious Trauma can adversely impact team communication, collaboration, cohesion, and coordinated responses

- Productivity-Vicarious Trauma can erode staff's ability to do their jobs effectively, specifically their ability to make decisions.

- Staff Turnover-Vicarious Trauma can cost agencies thousands of dollars in cost due to low staff retention. The cost for each worker leaving an agency and rehiring process.

First Responder worries can include their own personal history with:

- Trauma,
- History of Grief and Loss,
- History of Medical Interventions,
- History of Child Abuse: Sexual Abuse, Physical Abuse or Neglect
- History of Accidents,
- History of Natural Disasters
- History of Witnessing Acts of Violence
- History of Cultural, Intergenerational, and Historical Trauma
- Physical, Mental, Spiritual, Health and Well-being of their own families

- Ongoing exposure to trauma and traumatic events because of the ongoing work with families and the community.

As a society, we often rely on First Responders to be the first line of defense during emergencies. They are the people who show up first on the scene of accidents, natural disasters, and other emergencies. However, the nature of their work can take a toll on their mental health. It is important to maintain awareness of First Responders' mental health and provide them with the support they need. First Responders have a duty to themselves and the community to be strong mental health advocates. The policies in agencies that you work for should provide the following:

- Provide mental health training: It is important to provide First Responders with training on how to recognize and manage stress, trauma, and other mental health issues. This can help them better cope with the challenges they face on the job.

- Encourage self-care: First Responders should be encouraged to take care of themselves both physically and mentally. This can include things like exercise, healthy eating, and practicing mindfulness.

- Provide support resources: Make sure that First Responders have access to mental health resources such as counseling services, support groups, and employee assistance programs. This can help them get the help they need if they are struggling.

- Foster a supportive work environment: It is important to create a work environment that is supportive of First Responders' mental health. This can include things like providing opportunities for debriefing after difficult incidents, ensuring adequate rest breaks, and promoting work-life balance.

Ultimately, it is your responsibility to protect your right to healthy mental well-being. It is within the rights of all First Responders to maintain policies that protect mental health and providing them with the support they need, we can help ensure that they are able to continue to serve and protect our communities to the best of their abilities.

YOU DO NOT NEED ANYONE'S PERMISSION TO MAKE CHOICES TO GUARD YOUR MENTAL HEALTH.

LaLisa Morgan, Author

MINDING YOUR BUSINESS AS A FIRST RESPONDER

Minding your own business is a phrase that has been passed down for generations and for good reason. However, with the First Responder, one must maintain sound mental health boundaries so that you don't insert yourself in situations outside of work. This is a reminder that we should focus on our own lives and not meddle in the affairs of others. It is only when you are in your official capacity do you have to pay attention to information and environments that may cause you to take action to ensure safety.

You have a right to privacy, and by minding our own business, you demonstrate self-respect for that right. We should not pry into other people's lives or spread rumors about them. When we respect other people's privacy and avoid spreading rumors, we build trust with others. This can lead to stronger relationships and a more positive community.

Boundaries at work are very important. Some work environments are magnets for toxic behavior. When we get involved in other people's business, we risk being dragged into their drama. This can cause unnecessary stress and anxiety, and it can also damage your relationships with others.

It is important to invest in your own personal growth. When we spend too much time worrying about others, we neglect our own personal growth. By minding our own business, we can focus on our own goals and aspirations. By setting a good example as a First Responder, you are an example for others to follow. We show that we value privacy, respect, and personal growth, and we encourage others to do the same.

Minding your own business is an important aspect of being a responsible and respectful member of society. By focusing on our own lives and goals, we can build trust, avoid drama, and set a positive example for others to follow. I want to encourage you to dig even deeper. Your mind, will, and emotions are part of who you are. The essence of your being. Your mind, will, and emotions work together to shape your personality and guide your actions. They are integral components of your being, and understanding how they interact can help you live a more fulfilling life. To envision and elevate to the next level in your career, one must nurture and harness the power of your mind, will, and emotions.

- By practicing mindfulness, you can become more aware of your thoughts and emotions. This awareness can help you identify patterns of behavior that may be holding you back, and enable you to make more conscious decisions.

- Willpower is the ability to resist immediate gratification in pursuit of a long-term goal. Developing your willpower can help you overcome procrastination, build healthy habits, and achieve your goals.

- Emotional intelligence is the ability to recognize and manage your own emotions, as well as understand and empathize with others. By building your emotional intelligence, you can improve your relationships, communication skills, and overall well-being.

Remember, your mind, will, and emotions are powerful tools that can help you achieve your dreams and live a fulfilling life. By nurturing and harnessing their power, you can unlock your full potential and create the future you desire. You are not just a First Responder. You deserve to live your best life in relationships that allow you to thrive!! Success is loving life and daring to live it (Maya Angelou)! So, what you believe, and value is very important to your quality of life.

Core values and beliefs are the building blocks of an individual's character and decision-making process. They serve as guiding principles that shape one's perception of the world and their behavior towards it. These values are often deeply entrenched and can be influenced by various factors such as upbringing, culture, religion, and personal experiences. Here are some examples of core values and beliefs:

- _Integrity:_ The belief in being honest and having strong moral principles

- _Respect:_ The belief in treating others with dignity and consideration

- _Responsibility:_ The belief in being accountable for one's actions and their consequences

- _Compassion:_ The belief in showing empathy and kindness towards others

- _Perseverance_: The belief in persisting through challenges and obstacles

- _Equality:_ The belief in the fair treatment and opportunity for all individuals, regardless of background or identity

It's worth noting that core values and beliefs can vary widely between individuals and can change over time due to personal growth and life experiences. They act as a compass that guides individuals towards their goals and helps them navigate life's complexities with purpose and meaning.

Wellness is a term that has a different meaning for everyone. Fundamentally, wellness is more than just the absence of disease or stress - it encompasses overall well-being. It involves having a purpose in life, actively engaging in satisfying work and play, having joyful relationships, maintaining a healthy physical body, and enjoying a quality of living in an environment that aligns with one's definition of happiness. Wellness takes a holistic approach by considering the interconnectedness of various aspects of an individual's life, including physical, mental, and social well-being.

Substance Abuse and Mental Health Services Administration (SAMHSA) has defined Eight Dimensions of Wellness—emotional, environmental, financial, intellectual, occupational, physical, social, and spiritual—to achieve longevity and improved quality of life. To achieve wellness, there are eight dimensions that an individual should focus on.

These dimensions are interconnected and are all crucial to a person's overall well-being.

1. **Emotional wellness**: This pertains to an individual's ability to manage their emotions and cope with life's challenges. Emotional wellness involves being aware of and accepting one's feelings, having a positive outlook, and being able to express oneself in a healthy manner.

2. **Environmental wellness**: This dimension of wellness focuses on an individual's relationship with their surroundings. It includes having a safe and healthy living environment, being aware of one's impact on the environment, and taking steps to protect and preserve natural resources.

3. **Financial wellness**: Financial wellness involves having a stable financial situation. This includes having a good understanding of personal finances, managing money responsibly, and planning.

4. **Intellectual wellness**: This dimension of wellness involves continuing to learn and grow intellectually throughout life. It includes seeking out new knowledge, challenging oneself intellectually, and being open to new ideas.

5. **Occupational wellness**: This pertains to an individual's satisfaction and fulfillment with their job or career. It involves having a sense of purpose and meaning in one's work, feeling valued and appreciated, and having a good work-life balance.

6. **Physical wellness**: Physical wellness involves taking care of one's body through proper nutrition, exercise, and rest. It includes being mindful of one's physical health and taking steps to maintain it.

7. **Social wellness**: This dimension of wellness involves having fulfilling relationships and social support networks. It includes being able to communicate effectively, building strong connections with others, and having a sense of belonging.

8. **Spiritual wellness**: Spiritual wellness involves having a sense of purpose and meaning in life. It includes being connected to something greater than oneself and having a set of values or beliefs that guide one's actions.

"Motivation is a fire from within. If someone else tries to light that fire under you, chances are it will burn very briefly." Stephen Covey

First Responder Mindset

As a First Responder, your passion for the work needs to integrate your own core values. As previously mentioned, the eight dimensions of wellness can launch you into a daily practice that achieves your maximum level of success and mental wellness. Wellness is not just about physical health, but encompasses various aspects of life, including emotional, social, intellectual, occupational, environmental, and spiritual well-being. Through the process of mental health therapy, you can identify your core values and beliefs for each dimension of wellness. By learning to love you and understanding your values and beliefs, you can create a roadmap for achieving your goals and living a fulfilling life. For example, if social well-being is important to you, your core values may include building and maintaining healthy relationships, practicing effective communication, and engaging in meaningful activities with others. On the other hand, if environmental well-being is a priority, your core values may involve reducing your carbon footprint, being mindful of your consumption habits, and supporting sustainable practices. Once you have identified your core values, you can incorporate them into your daily routine through actions such as setting intentions, practicing gratitude, and reflecting on your progress. By aligning your actions with your core values, you can achieve a greater sense of purpose and fulfillment, and ultimately reach your maximum level of success. This book was written to support empowering First Responders to unlock their full potential for a healthy life-work balance. By focusing on these different aspects of life, you can improve your overall quality of life and achieve longevity. First Responders to unlock their full potential and achieve a healthy life-work balance:

1. ***Prioritize self-care:*** It's important to take care of yourself physically, mentally, and emotionally. This can include getting enough sleep, exercising regularly, eating a healthy diet, and taking time for hobbies and activities that bring you joy.

2. ***Set boundaries:*** Learn to say no to activities or commitments that don't align with your priorities or values. It's okay to prioritize your own needs and say no to things that may cause unnecessary stress or overload.

3. ***Practice mindfulness:*** Mindfulness can help you stay present and focused in the moment, reducing stress, and improving overall well-being. You can practice mindfulness through meditation, deep breathing exercises, or simply taking a few moments to pause and focus on your senses.

4. **Learn to delegate:** As a First Responder, you may feel the need to take on everything yourself. However, it's important to learn to delegate tasks and responsibilities when possible. This can help reduce stress and improve overall efficiency.

5. **Build a support network:** Surround yourself with positive and supportive people who can help you navigate the challenges of life as a First Responder. This can include family members, friends, colleagues, or even a professional counselor.

By implementing these tips, First Responders can unlock their full potential and achieve a healthy life-work balance, improving their overall quality of life and achieving longevity.

Balance is not about avoiding challenges, but about finding strength and resilience within them."

Author Unknown

BOUNDARIES FOR FIRST RESPONDERS

First Responders have improved quality of life with sound boundaries for maximum career success and mental wellness which is essential to establish sound boundaries. What are the boundaries? Boundaries can be defined as the limits we set for ourselves and others in terms of behavior, actions, and interactions. These limits can be physical, emotional, or psychological, and they help us establish a sense of safety, security, and respect in our relationships with others. Boundaries are an important part of maintaining healthy relationships and personal well-being. Boundaries can be different for each person and each relationship. What might be acceptable behavior in one relationship may not be in another. Setting boundaries can help establish clear expectations and improve communication in relationships. It can also help prevent misunderstandings and conflict.

Boundaries can be challenging to set and maintain, especially when we feel pressured to compromise or when others push back against our boundaries. It's important to be confident in our boundaries and to communicate them clearly and respectfully. When our boundaries are violated, it is important to address the issue and communicate our feelings in a calm and assertive manner. This can help prevent further boundary violations and improve the relationship. Boundaries can change over time as we grow and evolve as individuals. It's important to be flexible and open to reassessing and adjusting our boundaries as needed. Overall, boundaries are an essential part of healthy relationships and personal well-being. By setting and maintaining clear boundaries, we can establish a sense of safety, security, and respect in our interactions with others. Setting boundaries is essential for maintaining a healthy work-life balance and avoiding burnout. Here are some tips on how to set boundaries that align with your values and priorities:

What are the things that you absolutely cannot compromise on? By learning to identify your non-negotiables, you can also learn to protect your peace of mind. This could be spending time with family and friends, pursuing a hobby, or simply having downtime to relax and recharge. Once you've identified your non-negotiables, make sure to prioritize them and build your boundaries around them.

Communicate your boundaries clearly to others without feeling ashamed of your authentic self. It's important to let others know what your boundaries are so that they can respect them. This could be as simple as saying "I'm not available to work on weekends" or "I need to leave the office by 6pm every day." Be firm but respectful when communicating your boundaries and make sure to stick to them.

A big boundary is learning to say "no." Saying no can be difficult, especially if you are used to saying yes to everything. However, learning to say no is an important part of setting boundaries. If something doesn't align with your values or priorities, it's okay to decline.

Lastly, be flexible with the evolution of you. While it's important to stick to your boundaries, it's also important to be flexible when necessary. Life can be unpredictable, and sometimes you may need to adjust your boundaries to accommodate unexpected circumstances. Just make sure that any adjustments you make are in line with your values and priorities.

Remember, setting boundaries is about taking care of yourself and creating a healthy work-life balance. By identifying your values and priorities and building your boundaries around them, you can ensure that you're living a life that aligns with your goals and values.

In summary, people cannot respect your boundaries if they do not know what they are. Be clear and assertive when communicating your boundaries. It is important to say no when something does not align with your values or priorities. Saying yes to everything can lead to burnout and resentment. Prioritize self-care activities that help you manage stress and maintain your mental wellness. This could be anything from practicing yoga to spending time with loved ones. And finally, if you are struggling to establish or maintain boundaries, seek support from a trusted friend, family member, or mental health professional. Remember that setting boundaries is not a one-time event but rather an ongoing process. It takes time and effort to establish and maintain healthy boundaries, but the benefits are well worth it. By prioritizing your mental wellness and setting sound boundaries, achieve life work balance as a First Responder.

Boundaries can help First Responders when struggling relationship by having honest conversations, seeking counseling or therapy, and committing to making positive life changes. Building and maintaining healthy relationships can be challenging, but it is important to remember that it takes effort and dedication. Let's reflect on the following:

- **Practice active listening:** Communication is key in any relationship, and active listening is an important component of effective communication. Make a conscious effort to listen to your loved ones without interrupting or judging them. This will help them feel heard and valued, which can strengthen your bond.

- **Show empathy:** Empathy is the ability to understand and share the feelings of another person. When you show empathy towards your loved ones, you demonstrate that you care about their well-being and are willing to support them through difficult times.

- **Practice forgiveness:** No one is perfect, and mistakes are bound to happen in any relationship. Learning to forgive and let go of grudges can help you move past conflicts and strengthen your connection. The first person you should practice forgiving is YOU! Then, you can truly access the gift of forgiving other people.

- **Set boundaries:** Boundaries are essential in any healthy relationship. Be clear about your own needs and expectations and communicate them with your loved ones. This will help prevent misunderstandings and ensure that everyone feels respected and valued.

Remember, First Responder, the pressure work can cause relationships to be fragile. Relationships take work. However, the rewards are worth it. By taking the time to connect with your loved ones, show appreciation and gratitude, and make positive changes, you can strengthen and deepen your relationships for years to come.

Redefining or identifying your relationship goals: You can ignite your passions., you need to know who you are working for. Clarify your relationships by journaling and taking some time to think about your goals and write them down. This will help you stay focused and motivated as you work towards achieving them. Once you have identified your goals, the next step is to create a plan of action that will help you achieve them.

- Break your goals down into smaller, more manageable tasks. This will make them less overwhelming and easier to tackle.

- Set deadlines for each task to keep yourself accountable and ensure that you're making steady progress.

- Create a schedule or routine that includes time for working on your goals. This will help you stay consistent and make steady progress.

- Stay positive and motivated by celebrating your progress along the way. Take time to acknowledge your achievements and keep yourself motivated to continue working towards your goals.

Remember, by creating a plan and staying focused, you can make steady progress and achieve great things. Life without a plan, is a plan to fail. You must keep your goals in mind, break them down into smaller, manageable tasks. This will make them feel more achievable and help you stay on track. Breaking down your goals into smaller, manageable tasks is a crucial step towards achieving success. Here are some tips to help you with this process:

- Start by identifying the major components of your goal. For example, if your goal is to write a book, the major components might be research, outlining, drafting, editing, and publishing.

- Break each major component into smaller, more specific tasks. For instance, under research, you might include tasks such as reading books on your topic, conducting interviews, and reviewing relevant articles.

- Prioritize each task according to its importance and urgency. This will help you stay focused on the most critical tasks and avoid getting bogged down in less important ones.

- Assign deadlines to each task to help you stay accountable and on track. Be realistic in your deadlines, but also make sure they give you a sense of urgency to keep you motivated.

By breaking down your goals or tasks into smaller, more manageable ones, you will be able to make steady progress towards achieving success. Remember to celebrate your accomplishments along the way, no matter how small they may seem.

Sometimes stepping away from work can help you come up with new ideas or renew the passion for the work you do. Take a break and do something else, like going for a walk or spending time with friends. A nap can spark a creative idea, or a dream can create motivation. Keep a notebook: Jot down your ideas as they come to you, even if they don't seem fully formed yet. This can help you remember them later and build on them over time. Remember, inspiration can come from anywhere, so keep an open mind and stay curious.

To keep in line with your passions and life goals takes time and effort, so it's important to stay committed. Set aside time each day to work towards your goals, and don't give up if you encounter setbacks along the way. Staying committed is crucial when it comes to achieving your goals and reigniting your passions.

If you're looking to reignite your passion as a First Responder, remember your "why" as to the decision you made to become one. To keep this passion going, you need to understand that it takes time and effort. Staying motivated is key, so allocate time each day to work towards your goals. Remember, it's normal to experience setbacks along the way, but don't let that discourage you. Stay committed and focused on your objectives to reignite your passions and achieve your goals.

- **Set realistic personal and professional goals**: Make sure your goals are achievable and specific so that you can measure your progress along the way. This will help you avoid feeling overwhelmed or discouraged.

- **Stay organized:** Keep a calendar or planner to help you stay on top of your tasks and deadlines. This will help you manage your time more efficiently and reduce stress.

- **Time management:** One of the main causes of workplace stress is an overwhelming workload and tight deadlines. By prioritizing tasks and setting realistic goals, employees can improve their time management skills and reduce stress levels.

- **Communication:** Open communication with colleagues and superiors can help prevent conflicts and misunderstandings that lead to workplace stress. It is essential to express concerns and seek support when needed.

- **Life-Work Balance**: Maintaining a healthy life-work balance is crucial to preventing chronic stress. Remember, the reason people work is to they can live and love their families and community. Life comes first!!! Encouraging employees to take breaks, pursue hobbies, and spend time with family and friends can help reduce stress levels and improve overall well-being.

- **Support systems:** Providing access to counseling services, employee assistance programs, and wellness resources can help employees cope with workplace stress and promote mental health.

- **Surround yourself with support:** Seek out people who share your passions and can provide encouragement and motivation when you need it. This can be friends, family, or even a mentor.

- **Celebrate your successes:** Take time to acknowledge and celebrate your accomplishments, no matter how small they may seem. This will help you stay motivated and build momentum towards your goal.

- **Organizational culture:** Whether you are in management or a subordinate position, you can create a positive and supportive organizational culture that values First Responders' well-being and work-life balance is essential to preventing chronic stress in the workplace. This can be achieved through training programs, leadership development, and regular employee feedback.

Being a First Responder is a journey, not a destination. Stay committed, stay focused, and keep pushing forward. You've got this! Remember, the most important thing is to believe in yourself and your ability to achieve great things. With a little bit of dedication and hard work, you can light a fire under any aspect of your life and achieve your dreams while navigating the important work we do centered on safety and well-being.

Success is loving life and daring to live it.

Maya Angelou

FIRST RESPONDER'S SOUND MENTAL HEALTH PRACTICES

First Responders face a distinct set of mental health challenges, including high levels of stress, long working hours, limited personal time, and the responsibilities of leadership. According to the National Center for Post-Traumatic Stress Disorders, trauma affects five out of ten women, and six out of ten men, as well as six percent of people living in the United States will develop trauma symptoms at some point in their lives. Trauma can happen to anyone, and the symptoms of trauma are not weaknesses. It is our body's response to being over stressed, and shocked due to a life-changing event. Trauma exposure, like living in impoverished communities, institutional racism, domestic violence (intimate partner violence), and community violence are examples of trauma. Mental health is the most underrated and overlooked element of human success. Without proper mental health management, burnout becomes a looming threat. Negative symptoms may emerge, such as depression, heightened anxiety, irritability, mood swings, and constant exhaustion. Here are some additional mental health habits every First Responder should be practicing all (or most) of these mental health habits on a regular basis.

First and foremost, listen to what your body is telling you. Our bodies are in constant communication with us, but they don't communicate in our language. Instead, they rely on symptoms to convey messages to our minds. It's important to keep in mind that feeling uncomfortable doesn't always mean that you have a disorder. Your body may be signaling that it's dehydrated, malnourished, lacking sleep and exercise, or reacting to negative energy in your environment. The body is in constant communication with us. Unfortunately, our body doesn't speak our language and the only way to get a message across to our minds is through symptoms. Just because you're not feeling comfortable does not necessarily mean you have a disorder. Your body could be dehydrated, malnourished, lacking sleep and exercise or just feeling horrible because you are surrounded by a lot of toxic people.

Invest energy into getting enough quality sleep. A strong

correlation exists between sleep and mental health. If you struggle with mental health, achieving restful sleep may be difficult. On the flip side, not getting enough sleep can lead to mental health issues. To break this vicious cycle, prioritize quality sleep as one of your most important mental health habits. Set aside 7 to 9 hours of sleep each night and treat it with the same level of importance as a crucial meeting. The human brain requires 6 to 9 hours of nightly sleep, with 8 hours being the ideal target for optimal performance. Remember, if sleep suffers, everything else will suffer too. So, invest your energy into getting enough quality sleep.

Our body composition is made up of fat, protein, water, and minerals that come from what we eat. It's important to note that not all diets are created equal, and we should all strive to eat more natural, whole foods while cutting down on heavily processed ones. As First Responders, we often prioritize work over breaks and neglect proper meals and snacks. However, taking breaks throughout the day to nourish your body will boost your productivity and overall happiness. First Responders often sabotage themselves by refusing to take breaks to have meals and snacks. They want to be as productive and focused as possible, so they work long hours and jump from meeting to meeting without ever taking time for themselves. This is counterproductive. You'll be much more effective, and much happier if you schedule breaks throughout the day and make them a priority. So, instead of working non-stop, schedule in time for yourself to refuel and recharge.

Our bodies are designed for movement, and if we don't use it, we lose it. While technology has made it convenient to accomplish tasks from the comfort of our homes, we must make a conscious effort to keep our bodies active. By exercising (preferably outside) for at least 30 minutes per workout, three times a week, we can improve our productivity and efficiency in all aspects of our lives. Physical exercise is demonstrated to be one of the best ways to reduce stress. As a bonus, it is incredibly valuable for your physical health, especially if you exercise vigorously on a regular basis. If you have the option, try to exercise outside, with activities like walking, biking, or jogging. The fresh air and sunshine can boost your mood even further and minimize the impact of even your most stressful days.

Considering recent social distancing measures and

ongoing debates around mask-wearing, many of us are experiencing feelings of isolation. As human beings, we all have an innate need for connection with others. Mastering the art of connection is essential for success in life. If you are struggling to engage with others due to the pandemic, it's important to at least connect with yourself or a higher power daily to maintain that sense of connection. All humans have a psychological need to connect with others.

Life is an adventure, and one of the most important ingredients is to have fun along the way. Having fun doesn't always mean going out and partying; it can be as simple as spending time with loved ones, trying a new hobby, or exploring a new place. It's about finding joy in the present moment and creating memories that will last a lifetime. So go ahead, let loose, and enjoy the ride. After all, life is too short not to have fun! The opposite of depression is fun. We often get too consumed with our work life and forget the fact that the human mind has a need to collect new experiences. If you're making tons of money from your business but not experiencing enough joy and laughter, you can't honestly describe yourself as successful.

Attending therapy can be a beneficial step towards improving one's mental health and well-being and healing from trauma. As a First Responder, therapy is a proactive preventative measure to monitor your mental health. Therapy should be something you get to do like exercising or eating. You need therapy to maintain balance in life. Therapy is neutral communication with someone who is not biased to their opinion of your personal matters. It provides a safe and confidential space to talk about one's thoughts, feelings, and experiences with a trained professional who can offer guidance and support. Therapy can help individuals develop coping strategies for managing stress, anxiety, depression, and other mental health concerns. It can also help improve communication and relationships with others, as well as promote personal growth and self-awareness. It takes courage to seek help, but attending therapy can be a rewarding and life-changing experience. Therapy sessions are arguably your best tool in the pursuit of better mental health. You and your therapist can find the right combination of tools and strategies that can help you manage and improve your mental well-being. Your treatment plan adapts to your needs. The opportunity to attend therapy could be monthly, weekly, or twice a month... you and your therapist determine the frequency based on your stressors and symptoms. Together with your therapist, you'll explore your biggest issues, glean a new perspective on your life, and discover the best path forward for your mind and emotions. Even if all you do is talk openly about your feelings, sessions have the potential to be incredibly valuable. Mental health professionals are mental health experts who provide services to individuals, couples, and families to help them manage mental health issues. ***Check credentials as some coaches are not licensed therapists.*** In the age where everyone declares to be relationship coaches, parent coaches, or divorce coaches, licensed professionals are supervised by the State and best practices of clinical intervention. There is a code of ethics for ensuring the health and wellness of the public good. Licensed professional help includes:

- Licensed Clinical Social Workers (LCSW)
- Marriage and Family Therapists (MFT)
- Licensed Professional Clinical Counselor (LPCC)
- Psychologists
- Student Therapist, such as Associate Clinical Social Worker or Marriage and Family Intern

There are forms of professional help that are not therapist but can be helpful. They are:

- Domestic Violence Counselors
- Substance Abuse Counselors
- Psychiatrists (prescribe medication)
- Pastoral Care

Each of these professionals has a unique set of qualifications, and the type of professional you choose will depend on your needs. It is important to speak to a few professionals to determine which one is the best fit for you and your situation. Mental Health Providers will each have a style and clinical modality that they prefer to use. Therapists can be helpful in many ways. Therapists can provide a safe and non-judgmental space for individuals to express their thoughts, feelings, and emotions. This can be especially beneficial for those who may not have a support system or feel comfortable talking to loved ones. Through therapy, individuals can gain a better understanding of themselves, their behaviors, and their patterns. This can lead to increased self-awareness and personal growth.

Therapists can also provide individuals with coping skills and strategies to manage and overcome their challenges. This can include techniques such as mindfulness, cognitive behavioral therapy, and relaxation exercises. By working with a therapist, individuals can develop healthier relationships with themselves and others. This can lead to improved communication skills, better boundaries, and increased self-esteem. Therapy can also be beneficial for those experiencing more severe mental health conditions, such as depression, anxiety, and post-traumatic stress disorder (PTSD). Therapists can work with individuals to develop treatment plans and provide ongoing support. A therapist can be a sounding board to create improved communication in your relationships.

A vacation is a period away from work, school, or other daily responsibilities, usually spent traveling or engaging in leisure activities. It is a time to relax, recharge and explore new places, cultures, and experiences. Vacations can be short or long, planned, or spontaneous, luxurious, or budget-friendly. They can be taken alone, with friends or family, or with a significant other. Whatever the nature of the vacation, the goal is to escape from the routine of daily life and to return feeling refreshed and rejuvenated. Vacations are more than just a break from routine life. They have numerous benefits that make them an essential part of a person's life. Taking a vacation is not just a luxury, but a necessity for a person's physical, mental, and emotional well-being. Whether it's a short weekend getaway or a long international trip, vacations provide people with the opportunity to relax, recharge, and explore new possibilities.

It is important to take occasional breaks from always caring for others as a First Responder to go on vacation and unplug from the world. This can be tough for the most dedicated First Responders, but you need to trust your team to carry on in your stead. If you want to avoid burnout and live a healthy, yet still productive life, it's important to make your mental health a priority. While there's nothing wrong with ambition, dedication, and commitment to being a First Responder, you can't afford to let yourself slip into dark territory – especially when so many of these habits are easy to consistently adopt. Taking a break from work and going on vacation can be a great way to relax and recharge.

Here are some benefits of taking occasional breaks from working:

- *Improved mental health:* Constantly working and dealing with stress can take a toll on our mental health. Going on vacation can give us a much-needed break from work-related concerns, allowing us to relax and de-stress. This can improve our mood, reduce anxiety, and boost our overall mental well-being.

- Increased productivity: Contrary to what some may think, taking occasional breaks from work can make us more productive. When we take time off to rest and recharge, we come back to work feeling refreshed and energized, which can lead to increased motivation and productivity.

- *Better relationships:* Taking a vacation can also improve our relationships with others. Spending quality time with family and friends in a relaxing environment can strengthen bonds and help us connect on a deeper level.

- *New experiences:* Going on vacation can also provide us with new experiences and opportunities for personal growth. Whether it's trying new foods, exploring new places, or engaging in new activities, these experiences can broaden our horizons and help us learn more about ourselves and the world around us.

Overall, taking occasional breaks from working to go on vacation can have numerous benefits for our mental health, productivity, relationships, and personal growth. So, the next time you're feeling chronically stressed, burnt out and overwhelmed, consider taking some time off to relax and recharge.

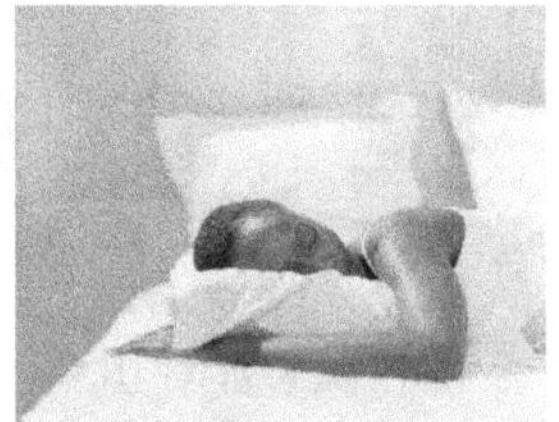

SELF-CARE IS NOT SELFISH!

You are intentionally making sure you are at your best to do your best work in the spirit of excellence!

LaLisa Morgan, Author

FIRST RESPONDER'S GUIDE TO LIFE-WORK BALANCE

As a First Responder, you know who you are—Doctors, Law Enforcement, Child Abuse Investigators, Fire Fighters, Ambulance Personnel, Nurses, Therapist, and more. You are the individuals who are trained to respond quickly to emergency situations. You are the first to arrive at the scene of an accident, disaster, or any other emergency. These individuals are trained to assess the situation and provide immediate medical attention or other necessary support to those in need. You are an integral part of any community and your work is invaluable. You give people hope to see another day. You put their lives on the line every day to ensure the safety and well-being of others. Your dedication and commitment to your work is truly commendable. In many emergency situations, the first responders are the first ones to arrive at the scene, often ensuring safety from harm or providing immediate medical attention. You assess the situation and provide immediate medical attention to those in need. This could involve administering CPR, controlling a bleeding wound, or stabilizing a mentally ill patient until they can be transported to a hospital. You are the ones who keep the children safe and may have to place children in protective custody of the state or county. You are the people who respond to disasters. You play a crucial role in responding to natural disasters such as hurricanes, floods, and earthquakes. You work tirelessly to rescue those who are trapped, provide medical attention, and assist with evacuation efforts.

You are instrumental in protecting the community. You play an important role in protecting the community. Police Officers, Child Welfare Social Workers, Ambulance Personnel, and others respond to emergencies and work to keep the community safe from crime. Firefighters put out fires and respond to other emergencies such as gas leaks and carbon monoxide poisoning.

You are providing emotional support in the community. First responders not only provide physical support, but also emotional support to those in need. You are the officer, therapist, or counselor who hears the first disclosure of sexual abuse or rape. You are often the first to offer a comforting presence and words of encouragement to those who have experienced a traumatic event. First Responders are an essential part of any community. Your work is vital in ensuring the safety and well-being of others. The world truly owes a debt of gratitude to these brave men and women who put their lives on the line every day to help others. Please remember you are never alone and even the helpers can use a listening ear, a big hug, and just comfort care. However, even if you're passionate about your work, the role of a First Responder can be overwhelming over time. Don't forget, you're only human. It's essential that you align with your core values and beliefs to maintain good health and healthy relationships. With so much to do, how can you avoid burnout? Prioritizing your mental well-being is key.

You may have continuous exposure to traumatic events and drama of the relationships (personal, social, and professional). These mental health challenges can cause your brain to be "addicted." These addictions manifest as negative mental health symptoms. You can be "addicted" to not taking off work and have a buildup of paid time off. You could be addicted to shopping and overspending. You may continuously be single looking for a perfect mate because of your trauma exposure.   You may lack boundaries with sexual interactions and serial dating. You could have been a victim of child abuse and your trauma manifests at work. You may be a perpetrator or victim of intimate partner violence as an adult. Such traumas cause you to be addicted to negative thinking, poor boundaries, low self-esteem, lack of self-care and several behaviors that cause you to spiral out of control. Pain impacts your heart, your home, and your habits in every area of wellness.

Admitting that you need to overcome these problems or "addictions" is the first step to making a change to the greater version of yourself. Examining your past is important so that you can overcome the minor setbacks in your life. These negative thoughts, ideas, and suggestions from the "stinking thinking" cannot be allowed to consume you. These negative thoughts need to be disregarded. The problems are crushing you and causing you to be weighted down from your greatness within. You want to change. You want a full and complete life. We all survived something. **To get to the life you want to live, you must endure the pressure that promotes that**

diamond life!! Some of us had to go through a lot of pressure!!!

As a First Responder, you are anointed for a higher purpose and calling in this life. Confronting the past, learning valuable life lessons, and loving yourself help you to evolve to the best version of yourself. You can embrace both your strengths and your weaknesses to be the best First Responder you can be. You can use this self-awareness to make improved choices to partner and collaborate with acquaintances, associations, and fellow partners in emergency care for your quality of life to improve your mental health as a First Responder.

As a First Responder, it's important to remember that your timeless sacrifice takes time and effort. Here are some tips to help you manage chronic stress, avoid burnout, and maintain your mental well-being:

- Set realistic goals: It's easy to get caught up in the excitement of starting to be a helper. To keep the passion for what you do, set unrealistic goals for yourself. This can lead to feelings of overwhelm and burnout. Instead, set achievable goals that align with your core values and beliefs. Write the vision and make it plain. Your career and family plan tells the direction of the blueprint or the map of where you are taking your life.

- Delegate tasks: As a First Responder, it can be tempting to try to do everything yourself. However, this can quickly lead to burnout. Learn to delegate tasks to others who can help you. This will free up your time and energy to focus on the tasks that are most important to you.

- Take breaks: It's important to take breaks throughout the day to rest and recharge. Schedule time for exercise, meditation, or other activities that help you relax and clear your mind.

- Build a support network: Surround yourself with people who support and encourage you. This can include friends, family, mentors, or other First Responders. Having a support network can help you stay motivated and focused on your goals.

- Practice self-care: Taking care of yourself is essential for maintaining good mental health. Make time for activities that make you happy and relaxed, such as reading, listening to music, or spending time in nature.

Show up as your authentic self. It is important to manage your emotions. You should demonstrate solid communication practices with verbal language that support your underlying needs. By remaining in your intellectual brain, and not the trauma, reactivity, or pain, you can embrace your gifts to maximize the opportunities to create income and generate generational wealth. By envisioning the best version of yourself, you can truly love your Creator, love yourself, and love your community ---family, friends, and your circle of support). You can't give from an empty cup. Taking care of you is a priority. Managing your time and creating a social life that allows opportunities to enjoy life. Managing your life-work balance allows time for your chores to be done, while creating time for family, friends, and community, and doing the things you love like hobbies and vacations.

Remember, your life a First Responder is a journey, not a destination. By prioritizing your mental well-being and aligning your business with your core values, you can create a sustainable and fulfilling *your* life purpose and bring your vision to life. As we close this chapter, please remember this valuable quote by Maya Angelou:

"You may not control all the events that happen to you, but you can decide <u>not</u> to be reduced by them."

You are in charge of your life... the captain of your boat...the president the corporation of "you".   You may have been exposed to a lot of traumas by being the first on the scene. Thank you for your serve. Now, walk in that authority so that you conquer the challenges which will be the present you give yourself. Do what you love. Keep pursing your goals, dreams, and aspirations. You are appointed to be the change you want to see in the world. Your kind words... your sacrifice of your time... your gentle care... or even just sitting with the many people you serve. You inspire hope in humanity, and it is uniquely presented by you**! You are a fingerprint of love on the Earth!** You are the most powerful forces in the world, and it is something that we should all strive to share with those around us.

Thank you, again, for your acts of sacrifice, and I hope that this book can continue to help you manage your mind while saving others. Keep inspiring hope in humanity with all that you do. We plant seeds for the future generations, so take care of yourself so we take better care of our future.

Your bravery is not measured in words, but in the lives you save.

Author Unknown

TYPES OF TRAUMATIC EXPERIENCES

The National Traumatic Stress Network has strived to provide definitions of types of traumatic events. There are differences between them based on the event, who was involved, and even the law. In short, you may have lived through one or many of these events. Here are descriptions of the core types of the types of trauma:

Sexual Abuse or Assault: Actual or attempted sexual contact, exposure to age-inappropriate sexual material or environments, sexual exploitation, unwanted or coercive sexual contact.

Physical Abuse or Assault: Actual or attempted infliction of physical pain with or without use of an object or weapon and including use of severe corporeal punishment.

Emotional Abuse/Psychological Maltreatment: Acts of commission against a minor child, other than physical or sexual abuse, that caused or could have caused conduct, cognitive, affective, or other mental disturbance, such as verbal abuse, emotional abuse, excessive demands on a child's performance which may lead to negative self-image and disturbed behavior. Acts of omission against a minor child that caused or could have caused conduct, cognitive, affective, or other mental disturbance, such as emotional neglect or intentional social deprivation.

Neglect: Failure by the child victim's caretaker(s) to provide needed, age-appropriate care although financially able to do so, or offered financial or other means to do so, including physical neglect, medical neglect, or educational neglect.

Serious Accident or Illness/Medical Procedure: Unintentional injury or accident, having a physical illness or experiencing medical procedures that are extremely painful and/or life threatening.

Witness to Domestic Violence: Exposure to emotional abuse, actual/attempted physical or sexual assault, or aggressive control perpetrated between a parent/caretaker and another adult in the child victim's home environment or perpetrated by an adolescent against one or more adults in the child victim's home environment.

Victim/Witness to Community Violence: Extreme violence in the community, including exposure to gang-related violence.

School Violence: Violence that occurs in a school setting, including, but not limited to school shootings, bullying, interpersonal violence among classmates, and classmate suicide.

Natural or Manmade Disasters: Major accident or disaster that is an unintentional result of a manmade or natural event.

Forced Displacement: Forced relocation to a new home due to political reasons, generally including political asylees or immigrants fleeing political persecution.

War/Terrorism/Political Violence: Exposure to acts of war/terrorism/political violence including incidents such bombing, shooting, looting, or accidents that are a result of terrorist activity as well as actions of individuals acting in isolation if they are considered political in nature.

Victim/Witness to Extreme Personal/Interpersonal Violence: Includes extreme violence by or between individuals including exposure to homicide, suicide, and other similar extreme events.

Traumatic Grief/Separation: Death of a parent, primary caretaker, or sibling, abrupt and/or unexpected, accidental, or premature death or homicide of a close friend, family member, or other close relative; abrupt, unexplained and/or indefinite separation from a parent, primary caretaker, or sibling due to circumstances beyond the child victims.

System-Induced Trauma: Traumatic removal from the home, traumatic foster placement, sibling separation, or multiple placements in a short amount of time. *(Adapted from National Child Traumatic Stress Network, 2008)*

If you have experienced any of these traumatic events, please consider a conversation with a licensed therapist. Licensed therapists include:

- Licensed Clinical Social Worker (LCSW)
- Licensed Professional Counselor (LPC)
- Marriage and Family Therapist (MFT)
- Associate Clinical Social Worker (ACSW)
- Marriage and Family Therapist Intern (MFTI)
- Psychologist
- Psychiatrists

Other Professionals you may find are:

- Pastoral Counselors
- Certified Peer Specialist
- Alcohol & Drug Abuse Counselor
- Domestic Violence Counselors

Remember, Coaching is NOT Therapy.

Get help from the right person.

COMMUNITY RESOURCES

Child Welfare Information Gateway (www.childwelfare.gov) provides resources for understanding Child Abuse and Neglect. Here are resources that Child Welfare Information Gateway provides if you suspect that a child's health or safety is compromised due to abuse or neglect by parents or other caretaker who has custody of the child, contact the child protective services agency in your county. Trained social workers staff these 24-hour Hotlines. If you are reporting suspected child abuse or neglect regarding children in another county, please contact that county's child protective services agency.

Child Abuse/Childhelp®
Phone: 800.4.A.CHILD (800.422.4453)
People They Help: Child abuse victims, parents, and concerned individuals.

Child Sexual Abuse-Darkness to Light
Phone: 866.FOR.LIGHT (866.367.5444)
People They Help: Children and adults needing local information or resources about sexual abuse.

Family Violence-National Domestic Violence Hotline
Phone: 800. 799.SAFE (800.799.7233)
TTY: 800.787.3224
Video Phone Only for Deaf Callers: 206.518.9361
People They Help: Children, parents, friends, offenders.

Help for Parent-National Parent Helpline®
Phone: 855.4APARENT (855.427.2736) (available 10 a.m. to 7 p.m., PST, weekdays)
People They Help: Parents and caregivers needing emotional support and links to resources.

Human Trafficking-National Human Trafficking Hotline
Phone: 888.373.7888
People They Help: Victims of human trafficking and those reporting potential trafficking situations

Mental Illness-National Alliance on Mental Illness
Phone: 800. 950.NAMI (800.950.6264) (available 10 a.m. to 6 p.m., ET, weekdays)
People They Help: Individuals, families, professionals.
Missing/Abducted Children-Child Find of America
Phone: 800.I.AM. LOST (800.426.5678)
People They Help: Parents reporting lost or abducted children, including parental abductions.

Child Find of America—Mediation
Phone: 800.A.WAY.OUT (800.292.9688)
People They Help: Parents (abduction, prevention, child custody issues)

National Center for Missing and Exploited Children
Phone: 800.THE.LOST (800.843.5678)
TTY: 800.826.7653
People They Help: Families and professionals (social services, law enforcement)

Rape/Incest-Rape, Abuse and Incest National Network (RAINN)
Phone: 800. 656.HOPE (800.656.4673)
People They Help: Rape and incest victims, media, policymakers, concerned individuals.

Substance Abuse-National Alcoholism and Substance Abuse Information Center
Phone: 800.784.6776
People They Help: Families, professionals, media, policymakers, concerned individuals.

Suicide Prevention-National Suicide Prevention Lifeline
Phone: 800. 273.TALK (800.273.8255)
TTY: 800.799.4TTY (800.799.4889)
People They Help: Families concerned individuals.

Youth in Trouble/Runaways-National Runaway Switchboard
Phone: 800.RUNAWAY (800.786.2929)
People They Help: Runaway and homeless youth, families.

About the Author

With over 30 years of professional expertise, LaLisa Morgan is a licensed clinical social worker, community activist, ally, trainer, mentor, and therapist allow her to support her clients to be the best version of themselves and heal from trauma, life limiting beliefs, deeply rooted family, and social barriers. Your personal development and your career affect your professional identity.

LaLisa is an alum of California State University, Los Angeles where she completed her Master's Degree in Social Work (2007), Master's Degree Health Care Management (2001), and Certificate in Applied Gerontology (1999). She completed her undergraduate program in Public Administration at California State University, Dominguez Hills (1998). In June 2022, LaLisa is an ordained to minister the Gospel of Jesus Christ, which was verified by the Dean of Ministries, Justin Blair at King's Company Ministry after completing ministry certificates in Pastoral Care, Prophetic Ministry, Deliverance Ministry and Christian Life Coach. In June 2023, LaLisa received an honorary Doctor of Divinity (doctoral degree) and conferred to be a Christian Life, Faith, and Marriage Counselor from United National Church. Additionally, LaLisa currently serves her community as a Supervising Children's Social Worker in Child Welfare for over seventeen years, ensuring child safety, building families, and strengthening communities.

LaLisa leads a rewarding professional career in the fields of child welfare, aging and disabled adults, and empowering youth in Los Angeles County. In her spare time, she has volunteered for several causes and agencies, such as National Coalition of 100 Black Women (NCBW-Los Angeles), International Association of Women Authors (IAWA), Azusa Women's Club, Commissioner of Human Relations for the City of Azusa, SEIU Local 721 Steward, and Academic Field Instructor for Social Work.

LaLisa has her own published books, including, "Surviving the Chaos: Journey to Healing and Legacy Living and companion Guided Reflection Journal," "Tales From the Hood: Tips and Strategies for Shared Parenting With a Person You Don't Like," "What Every Parent Should Know About Trauma," "Quick Explanations of the Role of Court, Child Abuse, and the Role of Parents in Sharing Custody," and What Black Parents Need to Know About Trauma." She has been included in several anthologies that include Entrepreneurial Women of Faith: Sharing the Scriptures We Use to Keep Us Anchored to, Focused On, and Motivated in Our Businesses (Book 1), Mothers, Daughters, and Faith (Book 2), Faith Is (Book 3), Pierced Into Purpose II, Boy Bye, The Healed Woman and Silent No More. She writes to encourage everyone to become generational curse breakers, heal from the past, and walk in wholeness as you master your individuality. As a Licensed Clinical Social Worker, LaLisa provides individual, family, couples, and group sessions for psychotherapy, coaching, and counseling for adults in transition, men/women individual therapy, and couples therapy to help develop positive coping strategies for anxiety, depression, trauma, unhealthy relationship dynamics, and working through life's peaks and valleys during life's transitions: young adult (18-30), prenatal and postpartum, parenting, and aging. In therapy, clients are genuinely "seen and heard" while cultivating change through insight and application of new skills. LaLisa has found that her divine purpose is to guide individuals to their life purpose as the therapy office is her ministry. Using the uncompromised Word of God, Therapeutic Modalities, and Self-Awareness, LaLisa helps others to achieve the best version of themselves and love of self so that they can live out their purpose with family, and community one person at a time.

www.kingdomjourney4life.com
Instagram: KingdomJourney2Healing1865
Facebook: @Journey2healinglosangeles
Contact Information:
Telephone: (626) 862-3837
Email: info@kingdomjourney4life.com

CREATE A CALM AND RELAXING HOME ATMOSTPHERE WITH NATURAL PRODUCTS
With doTERRA Products

What Does doTERRA Mean? Founded in 2008, doTERRA's mission from the beginning was to share the highest quality essential oils with the world. Having seen the incredible benefits of using these precious resources, a group of healthcare and business professionals set out to make that mission a reality. They formed a company and named it DOTERRA, a Latin derivative meaning "Gift of the Earth." The first hurdle they needed to overcome was to establish a quality standard in an industry that had never had one previously. The doTERRA founders were committed to providing only the purest, highest-grade essential oils. This commitment led to the creation of a new standard of quality: CPTG Certified Pure Tested Grade™. Every doTERRA oil is held to the highest possible level of purity.

Now, doTERRA means more than "Gift of the Earth." It means wellness, healing, and hope.

I AM YOUR WELLNESS ADVOCATE.

Do'Terra Wellness Advocate: Essential Oils, natural products infused with essential oil products offer natural solutions for you and your loved ones.
LaLisa Morgan, LCSW
Explore products and become a member today!
my.doterra.com/gen1865journey2healing

(626) 862-3837

OTHER BOOKS BY THE AUTHOR

Surviving the Chaos: A Journey to Healing and Legacy Living

Surviving the Chaos: A Journal for Healing and Legacy Living is a book designed to be read by all people on a quest for knowledge and wisdom, to heal from the mental pain or distress in their lives. By applying the Legacy Lessons that are shared by the author, the reader will empower themselves on a healing journey and build a foundation of their identity and purpose for their future. By reading this book, the reader will:

- Establish a new foundation based on your beliefs and values.
- Learn who you are and examine your past and what you need to heal from.
- Renew your mind by applying the seven legacy life lessons.
- Find your purpose by completing reflection activities and journaling.

Available on Amazon in paperback and eBook formats

Surviving the Chaos: Guided Reflection Journal

Surviving the Chaos: Guided Reflection Journal is the companion to the book, Surviving the Chaos: A Journey to Healing and Legacy Living. The journal is designed to help the reader reflect on the core principles discussed in the Life Legacy Lessons. By applying the Legacy Lessons that are shared by the author, the reader will empower themselves on a healing journey and build a foundation of their identity and purpose for their future. By reading this book, the reader will:

- Establish a new foundation based on your beliefs and values.
- Learn who you are and examine your past and what you need to heal from.
- Renew your mind by applying the seven legacy life lessons.
- Find your purpose by completing reflection activities and journaling.

Available on Amazon in paperback.

Silent No More: My Story, My Truth

The darkness in her eye represents her past. The light in her eye represents her future. The tear on her face represents the pain she endured. The story represents her freedom and healing. Silent No More is an anthology about childhood trauma. The authors are women who experienced horrific abuse and mistreatment when they should have been protected & cherished. They were violated, as minors. They were threatened to keep it secret and forced to keep quiet. Featuring Anjanette Robinson, Brandi Marsh, Carra Dixon, Danniel S. Withers, Jaynel Jones, LaLisa Morgan, Lucretia Y. Hayes, Melanie Rossum, Melissa McGill, Porsche Williams, Tanya DeFreitas, Vernita Edwards, and Lead Author Venus Chandler, with a bonus entry by Terry Chandler. As adults, these women are reclaiming their liberty and victory by telling their story, their truth. It's not an easy read, but it was not an easy journey to get to the place of being able to share what they experienced. Together, they are breaking the silence, and they are Silent No More!

The Healed Woman

The Healed Woman is the vision of two-time Amazon bestselling author, Browniesha Blackman, and it is a testament of 12 women who never imagined being broken, abandoned, and left to die in their mess. They each faced many challenges, yet they fought their way through. Now, they can say, "I was once broken but now I am whole. I once was in a trial but now I've triumphed. I once was in darkness but now God has brought me into His marvelous light.

The Healed Woman features a foreword by international, bestselling author, Tanya DeFreitas, and testimonies by the following women of faith: Browniesha Blackman, Ebony A. Smith, Edneisha Lee, Kadana Bryant, LaLisa Morgan, Laneice Joseph, Myisha S. Luebrun, Princess Mapp, Robyn Williams, Shae Clark, Tamika Jones, and Tinya Lewis.

Ignite the Greatness Within: Strategies to Maximize Success While Managing Your Mental Wellness

Book Overview: Ignite the Greatness Within: Strategies to Maximize Success While Managing Your Mental Wellness was written for businesswomen and authors to gain approaches to maximize success while managing real life with sound mental health practices. By addressing your own healing, you can greatly impact healing in your family and the community as a trauma informed business owner. By reading this book, the reader will:

- Define mental health and how professional and personal relationships are affecting your mental health.
- Learn about the different types of trauma affecting your business.
- Align your core values with your self-care plan.
- Set boundaries with family, friends, and business partners to build a healthy professional practice.
- Create your wellness strategies and maximize your income potential, business goals, and create the life-work balance.

Book Overview: Boy BYE! is an anthology featuring LaLisa Morgan and 11 brave women and a collection of poignant and empowering stories that explore the theme of ending unhealthy relationships. From toxic romantic entanglements to unhealthy marriages, the diverse range of narratives delves into the complexities of letting go and moving forward towards self-love and healing.

It is not just a book of stories; Boy BYE! is a powerful testament to the importance of recognizing when a relationship no longer serves you and taking the necessary steps to break free. Through its raw honesty and emotional depth, this anthology invites readers to reflect on their own relationships and find the strength to say goodbye to what is unhealthy and no longer brings them joy. Led by international bestselling author, publisher, and anthologist, Tanya Denise, Boy BYE! is a manifesto for women to prioritize their well-being and happiness above all else.

A program of Generations 1865: Counseling, Consulting, & Coaching:

KINGDOM JOURNEY TO HEALING

Therapy can help resolve and find solutions to life's drama and trauma!

- **SINGLENESS/DATING**
- **PARENTING/CUSTODY CHALLENGES**
- **PARENTING ADULT WITH SPECIAL NEEDS**
- **RELATIONSHIP ISSUES**
- **SHARED PARENTING & CUSTODY**
- **MANHOOD/FATHERHOOD**
- **CARING FOR AGING PARENTS**
- **LIFE TRANSITIONS**
- **SEARCHING FOR IDENTITY**

Are you looking to find solutions for life issues? A neutral person is often a non-judgmental solution to talking to friends and family. Therapeutic support can help support through depression, anxiety, trauma, or other mental health challenges. Relationship challenges effects mental health!

LET'S TALK!! Our program and services help you to make progress in life.

- Counseling & Psychotherapy for individuals, couples, & families to improve social & romantic relationships as well as individual growth, healing, and trauma informed care;
- Specializing in supporting Relationship Roles including Singleness, Couples
- Marriage/Cohabitation, Perinatal/Preparing for Children, Men's Wellness, Aging/Life Transitions, and Parenting/Shared Parenting Responsibilities

APPOINTMENTS AVAILABLE ONLINE (VIRTUAL)

Email, Call or Text for your appointment.

Program Administrator: LaLisa Morgan, MS, MSW, LCSW

Website: kingdomjourney2healing.com

NEED CLINICAL SUPERVISION? TEXT 626-862-3837

Matthew 5:14-16 MESSAGE

"Here's another way to put it: You're here to be light, bringing out the God-colors in the world. God is not a secret to be kept. We're going public with this, as public as a city on a hill. If I make you light-bearers, you don't think I'm going to hide you under a bucket, do you? I'm putting you on a light stand. Now that I've put you there on a hilltop,
on a light stand----shine!!
Keep opening up to others, you'll prompt people to open up with God, this generous Father in Heaven."